I0091151

Mother & Son

Also by Margaret Bolton and published by Ginninderra Press

Not Another Nun Story

Start with a Coffee (Pocket Poets)

Tales from Port Vic & other stories

Prisoners of War (Pocket People)

Mother & Son

Stories collected by

Margaret Bolton

Acknowledgements

Grateful thanks to all who told their poignant stories for this book.
I was honoured that you would share your lives in this way.

And thanks to Ray Tyndale for her proofreading.

Mother and Son is dedicated to my daughters, Nicki and Narelle,
and daughters-in-law, Celia and Kerrie,
all of whom have beautiful sons
and some of whom also have beautiful daughters.

Blessings on you all.

Mother & Son
ISBN 978 1 74027 771 6
Copyright © text Margaret Bolton 2012
Cover image © Rafal Olechowski – Fotolia.com

First published 2012
Reprinted 2015

GINNINDERRA PRESS
PO Box 3461 Port Adelaide 5015
www.ginninderrapress.com.au

Contents

Preface

Every mother has a story, a story that is worth the telling. How does one choose which to include in such an anthology?

These are stories of courage, grit and determination. Stories that give insight into the different lives of others – so that's what it's like to walk in another's shoes. Stories to ring bells – yes, I've been through some of that too, different in context maybe, but with the same will and the same love. Many of these mothers have faced huge challenges. They did this full on, and in the process, became the strong women that they are today.

Some of the mothers have chosen to write their own stories. Most of the mothers were interviewed either formally or by their sharing of their lives over the years. Because these stories are mostly told from the mothers' perspective, their sons' side of the story has not been included. However, all of the adult sons have given their approval. Some of the mothers have chosen to remain anonymous or to use fictitious names.

Losing Philip, Finding Adam

Margaret and Adam*

Losing Philip

I was going to Sydney to do some study anyway, and was about three months pregnant when I left Adelaide, so it wasn't obvious.

Armed with a letter from my local doctor I approached the large women's hospital in Camperdown to see what was needed in having a baby.

Regular visits were very impersonal; after all, I was only an unmarried mother. Often the doctor would bring along a troop of student doctors who also prodded and poked and listened through their little trumpets. Only the social worker treated me like a living person, but having my own flat and a job left her with little to offer.

By a very circuitous set of circumstances, I found myself visiting a psychiatrist regularly. He was helpful in pointing out my lack of self-confidence, but not in undoing that. He also helped me in actually coming to the decision for adoption. My aunt in Sydney was involved in a newly formed support group of women who were contemplating keeping their babies – one of the first groups of women to do so. But I knew that I wouldn't manage keeping him, especially as there were no Centrelink benefits at the time. And I had an ideal of a child being raised in a family with both a mother and a father. I made the decision deliberately and knowingly. There was no pressure on me to either keep the child or have him adopted. The psychiatrist was also helpful in preparing me to tell my parents about it all. After my aunt wrote to tell them the news, I went home to Adelaide when I was seven months pregnant, and it was very obvious by then. My young

* This is my own story.

brother greeted me with the comment, 'Gee, Marg, you've got fat.' My parents hadn't told him of my condition!

When the day of the birth came, I went to my aunt's place, and left my car there, while she took me to the hospital. It was mid-morning.

Philip arrived at about five p.m. after what I now know was not an awfully long labour. Although I had been to classes in order to stay with-it throughout the whole procedure, when the time came for him to arrive, the nurses took away my glasses, putting them out of my reach, so I couldn't see what was going on. And they put me out with their anaesthetic air, so I didn't see him when he was born. In fact, I missed the climax of the whole show. They wouldn't even tell me whether I had had a boy or a girl. It was a couple of days before they let me go down to the nursery and peer at him through the window. From what little I could see of a swaddled infant, he was beautiful, and slightly smoky in colour. But there was no holding or cuddling: that might create an unwanted bond.

There was another woman in my ward who was refusing to hold or feed her newborn child because it was the wrong sex. At least she had a baby! And it was strange being in a ward full of women with their babies and trying to avoid explanation of my lack of one. I guess the others thought that my uni friend was my husband.

Then came the day that I had to sign the papers allowing adoption. I was only permitted to choose the religion that my son would be brought up in, but knowing good Protestants and bad Catholics I let that pass. I did, however, ask that he keep the name Philip if possible. Immediately afterwards, I went to the public telephone box to ring my aunt to pick me up. This was the only place in the hospital where one could cry in privacy, so I sat on the floor and cried and cried, and cried some more, until some guy booted me out because he wanted to phone his girlfriend.

My mother flew over to Sydney to be with me for the first week. She too felt an incredible bond with this missing grandson which lasted for the rest of her life. She had once lost a child in stillbirth so vaguely knew what I was going through even though she never had the words to communicate it.

Six weeks later when I went back to the hospital for a check-up, the social worker told me that Philip had gone to a family who lived in a southern suburb and that the mother was older than me. However, she failed to tell me that it took all of those six weeks to find someone who was willing to have my baby, and so he just missed out on being put in an orphanage.

Dreaming Philip

As the years passed and I was back in Adelaide, I would often wonder how Philip was growing up. What did he look like? Who else was in his family? What sports did he play? How did other kids treat him? What holidays did he go on?

As part of a creative writing course, when the topic was a character description, I wrote what I thought a twelve-year-old Philip might have been like at that time. I guess I drew upon my own childhood and that of my children in envisioning his early teenage years. When I met him later, I was surprised at how near to the mark I was on several fronts. I even had him living at the suburb next door to the one he actually lived in, and while I had thought that he might have a great love of the sea, I hadn't guessed at his passion for surfing.

One evening a TV film reduced me to tears, not just a few, but tissue boxes full. Being in a similar position to mine and after great deliberation, a young woman had kept her son, only being forced by circumstances to give him up when he was twelve months old. My husband couldn't understand what the problem was!

And then at a church morning tea, a woman turned up with a four-year-old boy whose parentage was obviously similar to Philip's – a white mother and an African father. How I was longing to speak to her about my similar son, but I wasn't being public about his existence at that time, especially not at a gathering of church people. But the tight black curly hair certainly set the tear ducts flowing again.

I told my children about Philip and the circumstances of his adoption. I waited until I thought they were old enough to understand, about ten or twelve, and when an appropriate opportunity presented itself. Nicki had come to me one evening as I was preparing tea and asked me straight out whether she was really the oldest or did I have any kids before her. You could have knocked me over with a feather. I told her yes, and that I would explain after tea, which I duly did. At that stage she was daydreaming about the advantages of having an older brother. By the time it got to be Narelle's turn, I forgot to mention that he was probably dark in colour; I had become so used to the concept.

My husband had known all along, for I was pregnant with Philip when he first saw me. However, he was adamant that finding him wasn't an option. I think he was afraid that Philip might want to join our family. Later when we had a Filipino girl staying with us, I realised he had a problem with blackness of skin, regardless of the person inside.

Praying with the widow of Naim

In a period when I was dropping off someone else's kids at a local school, I would often spend some reflective time at a lake near the school. I was using a model of prayer that invited one to imaginatively get into a gospel story and meet Jesus as he was in the story.

One day I was praying with the widow of Naim, a story of a poor widow and her friends in a funeral procession to bury her only son who was a young man. In gospel times, a woman had no financial support at all if she was bereft of husband and adult children, and so was condemned to poverty or worse. Jesus took pity on her, came over to the bier and took the young man's hand saying, 'Arise', thus giving back to the woman a living son.

I, being the widow in the story (even though I had a husband at the time), prayed something like this: 'Don't be silly, Jesus, I haven't lost a son. What are you on about?' and then realised that I had indeed lost a son, even though it wasn't through death. And I knew in that moment that I would find him again; he would be restored to me. However, I also knew that I couldn't just sit around waiting for him to turn up. I would have to go and find him myself.

Searching for Philip

Media reports often highlighted the high incidence of deaths of young drivers on the roads. Philip was about seventeen at this time, and I was concerned that if I put off looking for him he might have become an accidental victim too. So I sent an eighteenth birthday card for him to Jigsaw, an agency that helped adoptees get in touch with their birth families, and vice versa, hoping that he might perhaps be looking for me too. Both parties had to approach Jigsaw in order to get a connection going. In the next couple of years, the adoption laws in NSW changed, so one party could actively begin searching for the other. Once found, the other party still had to agree to such a connection, but you didn't have to wait until they made the move. Amended birth certificates could be obtained from the NSW court system that gave access to the names of the child's adoptive parents. And so I obtained a certificate that had both the original Philip and the new Adam Philip's names on it, and the names and address of his parents when he was adopted twenty years ago. The Philip part of his name that they had kept brought tears to my eyes and the hope that things would turn out all right.

Finding Adam

Being a family historian, I was eagerly anticipating the search, which began in the phone book, and there they were, still living in the same house! The search took all of a minute once I had located a Sydney telephone directory. What to do next – a scary question!

After imagining how every scenario that I could think of might work itself out, and being uncertain of the outcome, I decided to use the services of a mediator in approaching the family. I went to the Relinquishing Mothers' Association here in Adelaide for help. But first

I needed to sort out some issues, and that was part of their role too. I needed to look again at why I had given up my son, for that would surely be what he might want to know. And I needed to look at the effects that all this might have on my own husband and children. And I needed to envision what likely outcomes might arise. What if he wanted nothing to do with me? What if his parents were afraid of such an approach? How would I feel and cope then?

The Relinquishing Mothers' Association sent a letter to Adam that was both vague and accurate in its content, referring only to the details of time and place of his birth, and saying that someone was wanting contact. They timed the posting of the letter so that it arrived on a Monday, giving him a chance to contact them and talk about it if that was what he wished. They didn't want him receiving the letter on a Friday when he might have had to wait the whole weekend to get whatever off his chest. He could even tell them to get stuffed, or ask them what sort of woman I was and anything else that they might be able to tell him. They sent it to Adam himself, not to his parents (I had fantasised contacting his parents first).

Adam told me later that when it arrived the letter was put on the kitchen table for him when he got home, and his father said, 'There's a letter for you. I think it might be from your birth mother.' So much for anonymity!

The three weeks that it took Adam to decide to get round to replying were perhaps the longest of my life. His response was to the Relinquishing Mothers' Association, but he had included a letter and photographs for me. I was at work when the phone call came telling me of its arrival and asking me to pick it up on my way home. I was so excited that I couldn't help sharing it with a workmate. She told me that she too had had a child who was given for adoption, but she had not wanted any future contact and she hadn't even named him.

My husband couldn't raise any enthusiasm to join in my joy, but my children were over the moon too. At least, the two oldest were. My youngest daughter was away with friends at the time, so we had another celebration when she got home. Her enthusiasm was somewhat dampened by the fact that I had forgotten to tell her that he was black, so the photographs were a shock to her. 'How could you!' was her reaction.

It didn't take me three weeks to reply! Over the next few months we wrote and then phoned each other, until I just had to see him. Adam kept making excuses. He was too busy. But they didn't sound like excuses for not seeing me at all, just delaying tactics. Finally I rang his mother and found a window of opportunity just after his uni exams were finished. I was on the next available plane.

Meeting Adam and his family

My seat was at the back of the plane, from where it takes absolutely ages to get down the aisle and out of the plane. I so badly wanted to push my way forward, jumping the queue. There was no trouble identifying which of those waiting were Adam and his parents, we had swapped many photos. Such hugs! And more hugs! And still more hugs!

I was armed with a pack of South Australian tinnies for Adam, who had told me that he liked to try as many different beers as he could, some South Australian wine for his father and a bunch of flowers for his mother. All of which were duly received. I couldn't take my eyes off my boy all the way to his home.

And when we got there, Adam and his mother presented me with a photo album of his life. What a joy to see him growing up and becoming the young man that he was. His mother had always collected two photos in case this day ever eventuated!

After going out for a special celebration tea, Adam showed me all his treasures: his sporting trophies, his school reports, his special toys from when he was a kid, posters of surfers.

The next day, Adam took me for a drive and a picnic to see the sights south of Sydney, his parents in the back seat. And I began to get to know them all a bit better.

And on the following day Adam took me to the Sydney Aquarium.

Studying marine biology at the time, he was a fascinating guide. I learnt such a lot, and peered through one of the windows of his world. Then we went to the Chinese Garden in Darling Harbour, where everything spoke to me so strongly of connections and wondrous new life. And it was here that the question of why came out.

It was a short visit, but how precious. I had wanted to buy Adam a ring but, not knowing him, had put it off. Imagine my surprise when at the airport he presented me with a gift of some beautiful Oroton earrings which I treasure and still wear often. So we talked about the sort of rings that young men wear and when I got home I found a nice one for him.

I sat on the plane on the way home, lovingly looking at the photo album yet again with streaming tears. I was the only person in my set of three seats. The hostess sat beside me to see what was wrong and shared my joy. I then found words for some poems (which appear below) and noted a feeling of restored wholeness now that my first born child was back in my life again.

Celebrating Adam

Six months later Adam celebrated his twenty-first birthday, his coming of age. He had invited my whole family but airfares for five us was beyond our finances, so just Nicki and I went. Nicki was working by then and could afford her own fare.

We spent the day time helping with preparations for a big barbecue in their backyard and getting to know Adam's older brother and sister and their families. At the party, Adam's father had asked me to get everyone there to sign a huge card for Adam – a perfect way to be introduced to his family and friends. And then he asked me to make a speech. Not being so eloquent, especially at short notice, I just said that I had been the first to know Adam and how special it was for us to be there celebrating with everyone.

Adam came home on the plane with us on the following day to meet all of our family. We too had a party, and my mother (his grandmother) even made him a cake exactly like the ones she had made every year for our children, a sponge with glacé cherries and cream on the top. And we explained the ritual of grabbing the cherries as soon as the cake was put on the table.

Even my husband came to like Adam!

What's in a name?

(for Adam Philip)

In days of old
on a high and thundering mountain
Moses came face to face
with his God
The God with no name
The God that was beyond knowing

But you, my little one
I have known you
You were with me
within me
such a short time
but for all eternity

In days of old
in a burning bush
Moses said to his God
But who shall I tell them has sent me
What is your name?
Tell them that I am has sent you
and that I will be with you for ever

And you, my little one
What name shall I call you
How will you know that
I am is with you
that I am with you too
for ever

In days of old
on a very small mountain
Jesus said to Simon
You shall be called Peter
for you are my rock
on which I place all my hopes

And you, my little one
shall be called Philip
for you need to know that I cared
and have carried you in my heart
just as my God has carried you
on eagles' wings

In days of old, my little one
in a beautiful garden
God walked with Adam in the cool of the evening
And now, my little one
I see that God has indeed
walked with Adam
all the day long

Cryin for ya, babe

I wanna cry for ya, babe
and hold you in my arms
When first you came I wasn't there
knocked out that they would cope with calm.

I wanna cry for ya, little one
and hold you to my breast
Those first few weeks without a mumma
just a nurse's white starched chest.

I wanna cry for ya, my boy
and caress your curly hair
For all the times they wouldn't play
'cos your colour's hardly fair.

I wanna cry for ya, son
and hold you very near
For I have missed you sorely
so far away, so many years.

I wanna cry for ya, fella
and sit you on my knee
And tell you how special you are
to Dawn and Dale, Arthur, Lee and me.

I wanna cry for ya, man
so lean and brown and cool
I see you tender, loving and strong
living life to the full.

I wanna cry for ya, Adam
in tears of streaming joy
How wondrous to find you again.
That's my boy.

You and I in the Garden of Life

This poem is quite raw, it was never polished.

In the beginning
God spoke but the word
and out of the void
all that is, came to be
In the beginning God created a beautiful garden of peace
Not so very long ago
humans built a manic city of concrete canyons

One day when first we met
you took me to a beautiful garden of peace
in the midst of the manic city
a garden of friendship
a garden that links

Beyond the portico into that garden
we walked
you and I
into the peace
in friendship
linked

It was a place of beauty
a place of tranquillity
a place overflowing with deeper meanings, barely perceived
a place to become one
you and I

Steps and stairs and winding trails
pebbled patterned pavements
pathways from the past converging once again
leading God knows where
for you and I

Gardenia, heavily pregnant with fragrance

Water cascading from rocky heights
saturating with life
old but not forgotten
new but hardly begun
longing to be known

Poised at the portals
windows and doors of life
invitation to a whole new world
the windowed patterns of so long ago
the patterns of our separate years
you and I
the patterns of the years to come

Water, quiet in a placid pool
reflecting inner peace
enveloping
you and I

Lotus blossoms floating
sparkling on the surface
the fullness of flowering
yearning towards transcendence

Golden carp
varying in hue from spotted pale
to opulent orange tinged with gold
completely at home among the lotus leaves
at one with their watery world
greedily gulping in suspended time
twenty years
you and I

Through the drooping willows
a cormorant perched on turtle rocks
wings spread drying
still
unruffled as ducks in pairs pass

Bridge, linking
rejoining what had once been
no more troubled waters

Bamboos strong supple and green
bonded into impenetrable thickets
hedging out raucous reality

Wondrous dragons, golden and azure
romping in the surf
playing with a precious pearl
Mythical, mysterious monsters
not ferocious in the way of the west
but friendly fortunate creatures in eastern eyes

And again water dripping over cliffed outcrops
a curtain of delicate droplets
soothing, caressing, refreshing
after the long search
you and I

Stately iris purple and strong
splashed with yellow
reaching proudly upwards
the king of flowers
direct yet delicate

Flat, black stacked rocks
dampness trickling down
like morning dew drops
gossamer suspended
catching rainbows in the rising sun
and holding them
promises for you and I

Graceful layered temples with upward curving waves
rich in decorated detail
reaching to meaning beyond
timeless
sacred is this place
today for you and I

The Fabric of Life

Anonymous

Every child is different. Every mother is different. What makes up the fabric of their relationships is unique. It is a history of shared love, experiences and life. A bit like a woven tapestry of a life story – or the making of a quilt.

When I was growing up with my four sisters and mother, I remember us all making a quilt of hexagonal pieces joined together to make flowers. We kept joining the flowers until we had made a quilt. Mum had made all our clothes and you could look at the quilt made of scraps from the dresses that she had made for us – and remember. Like a life story.

When I got married, I was hoping to have four children and I was distressed when it didn't happen. I was heartbroken at the news that we wouldn't be able to have children of our own.

We were staying with my father-in-law when I was told the news. I went home from the doctor's surgery crying. He asked me what was wrong. I told him and he said, 'Don't worry. You can adopt a child.' Looking back, I think he was the only person who would have said this to me. I certainly hadn't thought of that possibility. I didn't even know that it could be done back then.

So after we had settled into our new home, we put in the paperwork for an adoption. It was a hard time for me because two of my sisters were pregnant, each with their second child.

We had good friends at church, one of whom suggested that I mind her youngest boy while she was in hospital having her new baby. She suggested this so I could get some practice in looking after a child. All of our paperwork was approved for adoption and we were waiting. I was feeding breakfast to my friend's son in the highchair when the phone rang.

It was the Welfare Department saying, 'We have a baby boy for you. He's two weeks old. And by the way, does the crying child that I can hear belong to you?'

'No,' I said, 'I'm minding him, and yes, we are very ready for a baby.'

So I phoned my friend to take her boy to her, and went to collect my husband so that we could go to the hospital and pick up our new son. Wow, instant parenthood! A two-week-old baby, all our own. What a shock! I wasn't quite prepared for this. Then my husband said that he had to go back to work. Really! I was disappointed. I thought I'd be helped and spoilt. But no, I took him back to work and then went to my mum's thinking she'd get it right. But again no! She said, 'You're uptight. I'll feed him his bottle and you can make a cup of tea for us both.'

Afterwards, I left and coped with driving home with my new baby in his carry cot. It felt strange.

I did learn to manage and bond with him, after at first feeling so lost.

People commented that I had had it easy because I hadn't been pregnant, but I felt it was harder for I didn't get the support and fuss that new mums usually get when they come home with a new baby. Looking back, I think I tried too hard to be a really good mum because of the privilege of being given a baby to raise.

We took our baby home at two weeks of age. His birth mother had four weeks in which to change her mind about the adoption. This was a nervous time for us; I remember counting off the days till he was ours.

We then went before a judge at the Family Court to finalise everything. We had to swear an oath that we would tell him he was adopted before he went to school, so he has always known of his adoption. He came to live with us on 12 July; this is still a special day for me. We were issued with a new birth certificate in our names, and the paperwork to say that we had adopted him.

I felt blessed because two of my sisters had children the same age as our son, so he has grown up with lots of cousins. They have all been good friends.

We went through teething, croup attacks, chicken pox, all the normal things, kindy and school, tuck shop duty, puppies, cats and so on. So all in all the fabric of life has been woven as it is for all families.

I'm glad we had this experience as it makes for a family and for growing and maturing as people.

The Making of a Family

Denise and Martin and Cham

Denise and Ian had been married for several years but there was no sign of a baby on the horizon. As they both worked, they resigned themselves to saving up for an overseas holiday. After six months in Europe, they visited Sri Lanka. Denise thought that Sri Lanka was like a tropical paradise. 'It was lush and green and the people were friendly. The children were beautiful with their dark skin, dark eyes and white teeth. They would ask us for lollies or try to sell us something.' She was shocked when a young girl offered to sell to them her little brother who she was carrying on her hip. 'There was such a disparity between me desperately wanting a baby (and having the funds to obtain one), and her having to make such an offer in order to feed her family.'

As her maternal clock was ticking along, Denise thought it time to settle down from travelling and start a family. But still it wasn't happening. 'Numerous gynaecological explorations were performed on me, all with inconclusive results. So we went ahead and applied to adopt. We went through all the required interviews.'

Denise considered that adoption was a wonderful thing where both parties find their needs met and love is shared. She felt strongly that God had given her an acceptance of the role of adoptive rather than biological mother. But at the same time she felt cheated as she would have loved to experience childbirth. 'It seems to be a rite of passage for a young woman. It was because this urge was so strong that I got involved in IVF treatment at the same time. I found it to be a gruelling roller-coaster ride, what with being buoyed up with hopes of pregnancy, only to be plummeted down with disappointment. I did this six times. It became self-consuming, and I was near to a nervous breakdown.'

Then one morning came a phone call, but Denise wasn't at home. So the adoption agency rang Ian at work. He in turn rang Carmel, their neighbour, who had seen Denise drive out but didn't know where she'd gone. It was in the days before mobile phones and answering machines.

Denise continues the story: 'Carmel must have been aware of the importance of the call, for when I arrived home she accosted me as soon as I turned into the driveway. She told me to ring Ian ASAP. I did, and then I rang the adoption agency and made a time to meet our prospective child later that very day. Firstly we had to have a meeting to make sure that we were still wanting a child, and then we were handed a baby, who just slept through it all. It was surreal. After longing for this moment for so long, we were now holding a baby boy whom we had yet to come to know. I felt numb. Shouldn't I be bubbling over with emotions? It wasn't until we had been home again for some hours and the adoption agency called to see if we would still like to go ahead with the adoption that I finally let it all out. All I could squeak in reply was, "Yes, oh yes." We made some phone calls to family and friends and it wasn't long before the whole world knew. We had a lot to do as I hadn't prepared a nursery to sit and wait there for the eight years that it took. The next day we returned to the hospital for some more cuddling time with our new child. On the way there we decided on a name for Martin. I stayed in with Martin for the night while Ian came home and set up a nursery.'

Martin was six weeks old when they brought him home. Denise tells of a special moment. 'At about the time that he was born before I even knew of him, I had received a message from God – "All is in hand." That was it. Those words came to me as I was distracted by the most beautiful birdsong. I looked up and was surprised to see that it was only a common old starling singing. This really grabbed my attention because as a keen birdwatcher I had never heard such a beautiful song from a bird. I was amazed and took comfort, but had to wait six weeks for this revelation to come to fruition.'

Family and friends had been saving baby clothes and furniture for when the time came, and now they came flooding in. Everyone was as excited as Denise and Ian were. Especially heartfelt was the welcome the little family received the first time they took their new baby to church.

Martin quickly settled in and as he was a very sleepy baby it was a relatively easy transition into motherhood. The adoption agency, however, required that Denise have some training in caring for a baby, so they wanted her to go to Torrens House. There were no vacancies at first, so on the fourth day she went along. There she was surrounded by niggling and screaming problem children but all her baby did was to sleep through it all.

On reflecting upon the adoption process, Denise recalled that 'The Department of Community Welfare considered that, as Martin's facial features were similar to mine, they would place him with us. He also had a heart murmur – DCW had noted that I had been born with a hole in the heart. I needed corrective surgery at the age of two but thankfully Martin's corrected itself. So it was because of my heart defect that they thought I would have more understanding of Martin's problem. Martin did look as though he had some of our genes, and some acquaintances found it hard to believe that he was adopted. He even has a hairy mole on his arm that's surrounded by a patch of chocolate-coloured skin about the size of an egg, which is very similar to one that I myself have. Martin liked to compare our moles, as if it was a proof of connection.'

*

When Martin was about three, Denise and Ian looked to expand their family. By this time they had heard of couples adopting from overseas. Perhaps this way might entail a shorter waiting time, so they checked the list of countries from which babies were available for adoption and applied for a Sri Lankan child as they had fallen in love with the country previously. The same questions were asked of them at the interview with the Department of Community Welfare (in case an Australian baby comes up, was the explanation).

Only about a year later on a Thursday night they received a phone call from Sri Lanka. Could they please be there by Monday? Not much time, especially with a weekend included, for the last of the paperwork needed to be done, particularly getting a visa for the baby, as well as making travel arrangements. They also needed to decide on a name for their new child so that it could be put on his passport. They were, however, unsure of what his birth mother had named him. They knew it started with Cham but didn't know if it was Chamera or Chameira. Not wanting him to have an English name, they simply called him Cham.

Denise tells of the three bottles of port that they were instructed to take with them, 'to facilitate the adoption procedure in Sri Lanka. One for our hosts who would look after us, take us to appointments with doctors and immigration. The other two were for the lawyer who was not highly paid, perhaps because he was not well up on the legal procedures. Rather than having his own office, he worked in the corridor of the courthouse. And rode a battered old bicycle, which was somewhat of a worry since he had a drink with all the clients he visited and the traffic in Colombo was a maelstrom.'

The family was in Sri Lanka by Monday and on the doorstep of the Good Shepherd Convent in Colombo on the next day. This particular convent specialised in overseas adoptions of babies. And there they were given a beautiful but tiny baby boy to cuddle.

'Oh, those black eyes were so dark that it was almost impossible to see the pupils. They looked so black and liquid that I had the feeling of falling into them,' Denise recalls with fondness.

They learnt that his mother was a worker on a tea plantation in the hills who had fallen pregnant by the boss but wasn't in a position to keep her baby. She had come to the Good Shepherd Convent, where she knew that her son would go to a good home overseas rather than languishing in an orphanage for his childhood.

On every weekday morning, Denise, Ian and Martin visited the orphanage for about an hour, feeding and cuddling their new son and brother. They then spent the afternoon in a hotel swimming pool or playing tourists.

Still, it was not a sure thing that the adoption would go to plan. They needed to take Cham to a doctor for him to be checked out as healthy.

'If he did not pass the medical,' Denise says, 'we would not have been able to proceed with the adoption, and most certainly not bring him home with us. The next hurdle was for the adoption to go through the Sri Lankan court (when we had been there for a month). It could have all failed there – and very nearly did! We were there with the lawyer. Sister Dymphna from the Good Shepherd Convent was also there with Cham's birth mother, who looked so small and scared. We felt much the same. We didn't understand what was being said as it was in their language, not English. Then there was a delay and a commotion that involved Sister Dymphna, but at last our case proceeded much to our relief. Sister Dymphna told us later that our case was nearly dismissed as our lawyer couldn't find our paperwork in his disorderly satchel. She was not going to let the shortcomings of the lawyer disrupt our chances, so she quickly and boldly went through his satchel for him.'

They left a small gift for Cham's birth mother as a token of their gratitude, but were advised not to make contact with her as it was considered shameful to be an unmarried mother; her family could ostracise her and her prospects of continuing to work could be jeopardised.

Martin too felt very proud and happy to play his part in meeting his new brother and bringing him home.

*

When Cham was ten, the whole family took him on a trip back to Sri Lanka to see the country of his birth and to experience some of its culture.

Denise has written an account of this trip in the *World Families Australia Newsletter* in June 2002.

When we arrived at Colombo airport we organised a car with a driver for twenty-one days. We travelled as far north as Sangira, the ancient rock fort, and down to Kandy through the hill country, then back up along the beaches. We went to see Kandian dancers and fire walkers. We visited a tea plantation and factory. We went on a flying fox and a toddy tapping rope network high in the coconut trees at an adventure park. We saw elephants and crocodiles close up at a wildlife park. We had an elephant ride where Cham was the mahout and told the elephant when to go and stop.

We travelled in trains, buses, boats and tuk-tuks. We visited lots of temples, saw monkeys, water monitors, fireflies, squirrels and birds. We did lots of swimming, and much much more.

They visited the Good Shepherd Convent where Cham was living when they got him. Most of the staff had changed but the same nursery sister was there. She had been there for thirty-four years so she had helped in the adoption of over two thousand babies. They visited a boarding school to meet Umesha, a fourteen-year-old girl they were sponsoring as her father had abandoned the family and the mother could not afford education for her two girls.

Denise continues, 'We found the people friendly and welcoming. We had wondered how Cham would be accepted by other Sri Lankans, but there were no worries there. People asked why he was with our (white) family. I don't know how many times we told his story. People were glad that he now had a family and thought it wonderful that we had brought him back for a visit. Some people even gave him a small gift.'

The family found it interesting to see how Cham reacted to looking like everyone else, as at home he always stood out and was the centre of attention. Over there he blended in but when people spoke to him in Tamil, he couldn't understand them. They were surprised that he could only speak English, which is, however, widely used in Sri Lanka as a second language although its cadences sound different.

'It was good to see him being proud to be Sri Lankan. One of the first of many things that he bought was a Sri Lankan flag. And he got into the hot curries too – not to our taste. My greatest joy was to see Cham enjoy everything so much. He just revelled in it all.'

*

Denise summarises her experience of the making of their family. 'Although Martin and Cham were both adopted and we surely had our challenges and differences, I feel sure that it was in God's plan that we were to be a family. I thank God for Martin and Cham and believe that God wants to adopt each one of us into his family. What a wonderful thought that is! I'm also thankful for all the challenges I had in the making of our family as I think that without the challenges I would be a weak character, and may have just sailed through life taking everything for granted. That would be a terribly boring existence.'

Martin and Cham are young men now, but still living at home, a testament to the close-knit bonds of this family.

Out of Africa

Susan and Gareth

At ten p.m. on Tuesday 14 October 1975 in Durban, South Africa, a miracle took place. After seven years of marriage and repeated advice by doctors that they could have no children because of her medical problems, baby son Gareth arrived by Caesarian section. What rejoicing and thanksgiving there was for Susan and Eddie! How adorable was this child, and what nonsense was the counsel that a mother and son often didn't bond after a Caesar! Now they were truly a family.

Gareth was brought up as an only child, but Susan was determined that he wasn't going to be spoilt because of it. Even her mother thought she was too hard on her son. Susan took on after-school care so that she could continue to be a stay-at-home mum and still earn a small income. This gave Gareth an instant set of siblings with whom he could learn to play, share and resolve fights, and who could make up a cricket or a soccer team and celebrate lots of birthday parties with chocolate cakes topped with sprinkle icing.

As he reached the teenage years, Gareth went through that time when mothers could be an embarrassment. He insisted that his mother walk four steps behind him in the shops when she came to give her invited approval and credit card details for the purchase of new clothes.

Susan says, 'Gareth referred anything intellectual to his father while I looked after his heart and his love life. And I always woke up ten minutes before he was due home late at night, much against Gareth's insistence that I wasn't to wait up.'

Gareth was brought up in a country where apartheid was the norm. Under this government system the rights of the majority non-white inhabitants were suppressed and minority rule by white people was maintained. People were classed as white, black, coloured or Indian, and were discouraged from mixing. Schools, medical care and even beaches were segregated – black people received inferior services to those of white people.

Gareth was brought up in a family that believed that all people were equal no matter their colour, sex, religion and so on. As Susan explains, 'For our family there were absolutely no second-class citizens. I belonged to a group Women for Peaceful Change Now, and became the national president for the Anglican Mothers' Union, a worldwide organisation that catered for the needs of mothers of every colour, class and creed. Our family mixed with all sorts of people and Gareth learnt to mingle quite comfortably.'

Gareth grew up in a country that expected its young men to do compulsory national service, beginning in the year after they finished school. To refuse entailed a three-year gaol term. That was the reality of the situation the family faced. Susan elaborates. 'National service was for whites only, and once in the army, young men were expected to go into the black townships and keep order, sorting out the violence that was inevitable under such a system. The army's job was to defend apartheid, a lifestyle that our family was utterly opposed to. How could Gareth be part of something that threatened the blacks, many of whom we counted as our friends? It was an untenable situation. We could see no future for our son in South Africa.'

So when Gareth was fifteen in December 1990, they decided to emigrate, a couple of years before he completed his schooling. They came to Adelaide, where Susan's sister and brother already lived. They found a home to rent and a school that Gareth settled into quite quickly. He was bright in his classes, athletic in his sports, steadfast in his faith and generally made friends with people despite his accent. The other kids were soon calling him Gaz.

'I readily found a clerical job,' Susan continues, 'but Eddie joined the queue of more than a thousand unemployed engineers in South Australia in the time of 'the recession that we had to have'. He just simply could not find a job, so he began manufacturing towel-rail stands, at first in the garage at the back of his house and then in a hired shed in a small business manufacturing complex. After five years of toughing it out on dwindling financial resources, Eddie received a job offer in South Africa and decided to give it a go. After three more months, I joined him. We left Gareth behind with the front door key and the car, and returned to the home of our birth in 1995. Gareth was left to shop and cook, wash and clean, and to keep house for himself while embarking on a university course. This would have been unheard of in South Africa, where servants did such chores.'

The political situation in South Africa had changed by 1995. Apartheid had been dismantled and Nelson Mandela was the new president. However, now it was mainly black criminal elements that reigned, and security was a dominant concern for white people. They lived in their houses with electric fencing or razor wire around their properties for protection, installed deadlocks on the doors of houses and cars and some people even stopped wearing jewellery in public places.

'But,' as Susan said, 'nothing could compare with the heartbreak of leaving Gareth behind.' Every week they phoned him for an hour and eagerly awaited frequent faxes. Every year in the uni holidays either they came and visited Adelaide or Gareth went to visit Durban. Susan says that they saw far more of Australia and South Africa on these visits than they had ever done previously. They came to Adelaide for his twenty-first birthday celebration armed with posters for an Out of Africa theme, especially a giant-sized pin-up of Nelson Mandela. Christmas was always a difficult time, with Susan not even wanting to celebrate without their son.

Not being present for Gareth's two graduations, his bachelors and his masters, nearly broke their hearts. Susan was grateful that her sister Pauline Kelly, and her family, took Gareth under her wing every Thursday night for tea when she fed him fish 'for his brain', albeit disguised with a huge variety of sauces. Her sister took credit for him doing so well in his final exams! Her brother Christopher Russell, and his family, also stepped in and cared for him with regular meals and friendship.

Seven years later in 2002, when Eddie was offered a job in Adelaide by the guy who had bought his machinery when he left, he eagerly accepted and they came back again, to everyone's joy. By now Gareth was teaching in a Christian school and actively involved in his church community. He had served as chaplain at his alma mater while at university. He had a steady girlfriend whom he later married, much to his parents' delight.

'And it wasn't long before Eddie and I had a beautiful grandson, who calls me Gogo (pronounced GawGaw), the Zulu term for grandmother.'

Sadly, Eddie died in 2008. It was Gareth who gave the eulogy, a powerful speech of Christian witness to his father, whose philosophy in life was always to have 'someone to love, something to do and something to look forward to'.

And what a tower of strength Gareth and his family have been for Susan as she has struggled with learning to live on her own again. She now has two beautiful grandsons, Noah and Luke (who call her Gogo), and a loving daughter-in-law, Halina, who is not embarrassed to shop with her!

Losing a Son

Joyce and Peter*

The wind was ripping across the sandy shores of Golden Bay. A howling westerly was reaching its peak. To the south of the beach a rocky headland jutted into the pounding waves. Two ten-year-olds, Peter and his mate, were buffeted by the gale as they fished off the reef at the base of the cliffs. It was still early on a Saturday morning and they hadn't caught much yet, just a few tiny whitefish, hardly enough to take home for a feed. Even casting their lines was fraught with difficulty in the high winds. But it was great fun battling the elements like this, even though they sensed danger, so they kept well back from the edge of the thundering sea.

Suddenly out of the blue a humungous crashing and breaking wall of water knocked Peter off his feet and dragged him quick as a wink into the churning white water. Several fast following waves smashed him again and again onto the rough rocks. He just didn't stand a chance.

Peter's mate was utterly paralysed; he couldn't believe his eyes or comprehend what was happening. There was no way that he could dive in and save Peter; he couldn't even swim. For that matter, nor could Peter. When reality hit him, he turned his back on the thrashing sea and raced across the rocky platform, up the road past the cement works to the tiny settlement where all the cement workers and one lone farmer lived. Screaming his head off, he soon attracted the attention of some of the men not at work that day. They raced back with him to the spot where his fishing rod and yellow bucket still lay. Mr Scott was the one who pulled Peter out, battered and bleeding, with broken bones hanging at odd angles, and quite lifeless.

* It was Wendy who told this story to me. Wendy was Peter's little sister, a few months past her fifth birthday at the time.

A gathering procession made its way up the road to Peter's house, fearing his mother's reaction. Neighbouring women joined the procession running and gasping in disbelief. Someone ran to fetch Mick, Peter's father, who was out on his farm mending fences that his sheep had broken once again.

Joyce came down the front steps to see what was going on, with her mixing bowl in the crook of one elbow and waving a wooden spoon with the other hand, for she was making bread for the boys' lunch. When she recognised the pitiful lump coming in her gate in the arms of her neighbour, she let out such a piercing wail that few would ever forget it. Mrs Scott carefully relieved her of the bowl and spoon while other women and soon Mick took her into their arms so that she was surrounded by a protective wall. What could they say to this hysterical woman? Mr Scott laid the mangled body on the spare bed in Wendy's room; blood and mangled flesh soaked into the cream cotton quilt. Mick lowered the blinds, then knelt down beside the bed, covered his face with his hands and howled great tears of pain.

Joyce's neighbour quickly took the two younger children home to her place, to save them from distress. Five-year-old Wendy could feel the waves of agony and grief but didn't have a clue what was happening. She wasn't told that her big brother had just died.

The next day, relatives began arriving at Mick and Joyce's house – grandparents, aunties, uncles and cousins. Wendy had no idea why all these people suddenly appeared; she was still at the neighbour's house but could see them all going up the front steps into her home. Joyce remained shut in her bedroom, her eyes a constant red from the whimpering and crying: Peter was her beloved son, a blessed and welcome miracle after having two stillborn babies. And now he too was taken away. It was more than any mother could bear.

And on the day of the funeral, a calm but grey and cold day, Mrs Scott, from further down the road, took the two younger children for a drive around the point at the northern end of the bay where the sea was flat and gently lapping the sandy beach, and brought them home after the small white coffin had been lowered into the earth at the local cemetery, to join the crowd that had gathered for a cuppa.

Wendy came home into the kitchen, where all the cups and saucers were laid out and many women bustled about with plates of food. What was going on? Her mother wasn't in sight. Joyce was totally unable to be present, except bodily, to the crowd of people who had gathered at the home for the funeral.

Grandma Hawkins took Wendy into her arms and gently told her to go to her mother, but Wendy couldn't find her mother in the room. Joyce's beautiful auburn hair that had been so distinguishing in her ballerina days of old had gone completely white so that Wendy didn't recognise her.

At the funeral an aunt of Joyce's gave her a book. 'It might help, dear,' she said. Joyce noted the title *This is my son*, by Joan Kinmont, and had a quick look inside – 'You were the sum of all my inmost dreams, you were the ache and longing in my heart.' While the words truly reflected Joyce's feelings, it was more than she could bear. With an almighty wail she chucked it behind the sofa as she sank to the floor in more floods of tears.

At school the next day at morning talk time, Wendy told the class what had happened, how her brother had gone away, and many crying people had come to their house to drink cups of tea, but before she could tell them that her mother's hair had changed colour, the teacher reached for the strap, giving Wendy two sharp cuts to her legs. Wendy didn't understand that no one in this settlement talked about such events in public, especially younger sisters who didn't know what they were talking about.

A few days later, the whole family packed up and went to Timaru to stay with Joyce's sister and her family. But eventually they had to go home, life had to be lived again, it couldn't be escaped for ever; the sheep needed tending, the chooks needed feeding and the cows needed milking. After three weeks they went home again.

On the next Sunday, and every Sunday after that, Peter's family went to church and then walked straight to the cemetery on the hillside, where they placed glass jars of freshly picked flowers in a cross shape at the foot of the little wooden sign that had 'Peter' written on it. Wendy still didn't know that her absent brother was in the ground under the flowers.

*

Life had changed. Joyce seldom stopped crying, and was quite unable to cook and clean and take her children into her lap for cuddles and stories, as mothers do. 'She's had a breakdown,' her father explained.

Her brother changed too, he no longer had a friend, no one to play with. Peter's clothes and toys disappeared, photographs were removed; it was as if Peter had never existed, but still no one spoke of it at all. Both children had to do jobs on the farm for nearly every daylight hour that they were home to keep out of Mum's way. Dad was constantly irritable and grew distant. It felt as though the family was breaking apart.

Several years later when Wendy understood what death and drowning meant, she had a friend for tea. The friend noticed that her napkin was placed in a silver serviette ring with the initials PLS on it. She asked Wendy who PLS was. 'He was my brother,' Wendy replied, but before she could offer any further information, Joyce butted in. 'He's away at boarding school,' she said.

You Are What You Eat

Louise and Darren*

Darren was a classically hyperactive child. From when he was a tiny baby he never kept still but wriggled non-stop while awake, and especially when having his nappy changed. 'Once he started to walk, he was constantly on the go', said Louise. 'We lost several kilos in chasing him and trying to catch him for essential services. When he got to riding his ride-on car, he wore out a path in the carpet round the hallway. I had to hide round a corner to be able to give him some food or take off a jumper as he whizzed past.'

By the age of three, Darren often seemed to be inexplicably miserable. He always wanted what he couldn't have, had trouble getting along with other children and found it difficult to settle to sleep. Louise got quite frustrated when nothing she could do would make him happy.

She took him to a playgroup, where she encountered another child with similar traits. Here she learnt that the Fiengold diet had helped this other mother deal with her child. The Fiengold diet eliminates synthetic colours, flavours and preservatives, artificial sweeteners and food rich in salicylates like tomatoes, apples and almonds. In the days of the early eighties before food labelling and the internet, it was difficult to find which foods were free from these ingredients. Like a minefield, at first results were a bit of a hit or miss proposition.

Louise found that low blood sugar levels could also lead to behaviour problems. She vividly remembers, 'One day Darren slept in till late and missed brekky. He ran madly round in circles shouting loudly as he went. I had to give him a slice of bread as he raced past. As he ate it and his blood sugar level rose, he calmed down, walked

* Fictitious names have been used in this story.

41

quietly inside and sat down to his breakfast.' She had to keep a supply of snacks ready at all times, especially in the car for on the way home from school. Appropriate nibbles and a jug of home-made lemon drink were always available in the fridge for Darren to help himself. And at the other end of the scale, too much sugar also had its problems.

The Hyperactivity Association was especially helpful in undertaking research into various foods and publishing its results in a newsletter. It was the Association that alerted them to the fact of a sudden change in the ingredients of cocoa – brown colouring was added to one variety for a while – and advised them which brands were still good. Eventually Louise volunteered on a help line for the Association for, as she put it, 'I knew what it was like to feel alone with a child that nobody else seemed to understand.'

Eating the right things worked out all right at home, but when out or Louise absent, Darren had to learn for himself what he could or couldn't eat. But he knew that he felt better and behaved better when he avoided wrong foods, so that he wasn't in trouble quite so much. Friends' mothers soon got the message about what kinds of food were suitable. As he got older, if Darren realised that he had eaten some wrong food, he would often shut himself in his room, where he knew he couldn't pester anyone.

Louise continued, 'School presented its own eating problems, like when the canteen ladies forgot to omit tomato sauce on his hotdog, or the day he tried one of those new nashi pears (ordinary pears were fine, but a nashi pear is really an apple). Just a quarter of the pear set him off. He followed that up later at home the same afternoon by forbidden lollies, and took himself off to his room. It wasn't until I found the wrappers under the bed that I realised what the trouble was. On one of his sojourns in his room, his brother's violin playing annoyed him. Paul refused to stop his practice so Darren angrily banged his fist on the door. The door came off the poorer, with a hole in it.'

When he ate the wrong things at school, Darren's behaviour

quickly became unacceptable. He wouldn't settle to work, he'd distract other children or sometimes break into violent outbursts. He initially had trouble reading. It wasn't easy for him to follow the words across the page.

'Being a primary teacher myself,' Louise explained, 'I found ways to help him throughout school. In a new class at the beginning of one year, I invited the two team teachers home for a cuppa, so that I could explain to them the ins and outs of managing a hyperactive child and they could see for themselves what Darren was capable of when in control. That was a good year.'

The Mongolian BBQ became a favourite eating place for family special occasions, for there you could choose your own ingredients and flavourings and the cook would fix it for you on a huge barbecue plate.

And Darren showed allergic and behavioural reactions in the presence of many chemicals. Louise's use of soap, washing powder and other cleaners, along with fly spray, all had to be modified. She never used perfume or hairspray.

In days when smacking children was frowned on, Louise found that a good sharp smack on the legs helped Darren to control his own behaviour. This is akin to the slap on the face that is often given to bring people out of hysterical incidents.

Being at a loose end was never helpful for Darren. But he was a creative child, always hatching up new schemes for games with his younger brother. Louise and Kevin took care to provide a backyard environment that stimulated creativity. Large cardboard boxes, a sandpit and a cubby, some climbable trees, a place for the pigeons to nest, gardening plots – they all took over the lawn area. One of their favourite summer games was to use a water pistol for target practice on the shed wall or to shoot bubbles.

Louise continued, 'As Darren was somewhat uncoordinated in the sports arena, I had to look for activities that would suit. To help with his self-esteem, he needed activities that were special to him, that his brother didn't do. Darren learnt to paint with success at Ruth Tuck's art school. He painted out his frustrations with his current school teacher in the form of hideous monsters. He tried drama classes at one time. Hockey was his favourite sport at secondary school, as players could run exuberantly up and down the field chasing the ball without having to shoot for goals too often. I remember a day when our car had a problem that was fixed with some acrylic substance. On the way to hockey, this chemical affected Darren, so that during the match he lost his temper with another player and took an unsuccessful swipe at him with his hockey stick. And he swore at the umpire when taken to task over it. Sent off with a red card and banned for two matches, this sort of behaviour wasn't at all in Darren's normal repertoire.'

Holiday activities had to be carefully planned too. It was important for Darren to use up his energy, to do energetic things. On a trip to a road safety school, where children rode their bikes around a course that taught them the rules and courtesies of the road, at the break when offered the customary Coke, Darren said no thank you, he'd prefer water. But they gave him tap water (at home he drank tank water). The chemicals in it set him off on another round of unacceptable behaviour.

Water in swimming pools was also a problem. Reaction to chlorine showed itself in rashes as well as behaviour. So swimming lessons were a no-no too.

Louise explained about a facet of holidays. 'Preparation to do something different often had to be started early. Darren liked routine and the known. Part of his feeling insecure was that he found new experiences difficult and tried to avoid them where possible. It could take weeks to convince him that a holiday trip would be a good idea.'

Going to sleep was never easy for Darren, especially if he awoke in the night. Taped stories that he could listen to would provide a diversion when he worried about going back to sleep again – a 'good' noise compared to the scary creaks and thumps of night time. Later in life, Darren was part of a trial to test the efficacy of primrose oil as a soporific. He did sleep better when on it.

A firm teacher who provided firm guidelines and was able to interest children in many subjects was the type that Darren thrived under. When it came to secondary school, Louise and Kevin chose a new school that initially had only a small number of students. 'I made a pact with the home teacher, who would surreptitiously place a graded letter in his diary for Darren's daily behaviour. C+ or higher rewarded Darren with an interesting activity after school. Not only did it help Darren be more aware of his behaviour and its effects on others and so enable him to mature in this area, but it also made the teacher more aware of just how many good days Darren managed to have. It was a win-win situation. Only once did Darren attempt to change the letter before I read it.'

Louise and Kevin continued to read to their boys long after most parents would give up. 'I'd get Darren to read aloud the first page, then I'd finish the chapter. The problem with remedial reading was that though Darren's level of ability was lower than average, his level of interesting subjects was high. Books simply didn't cater for such situations. *The Chronicles of Narnia, The Hobbit* and *The Lord of the Rings* along with Terry Pratchett novels were all favourite books for Darren. They just don't come in easy-reading formats. Eventually Darren became an avid reader, but it took a long time.'

Darren repeated Year 9 against the advice of the teachers. 'But, slightly smaller in stature than most of his peers, this turned out to be a good move and gave him a sound grounding before moving on instead of continually floundering in the next level up,' his mother explained.

Darren found it difficult to learn things by rote. Spending hours at home with him in reciting the periodic table, it wasn't long before his four-years-younger brother could spout it off perfectly.

Louise dissuaded Darren from getting an after-school job; he had enough on his plate without that extra activity. In some ways she came to regret that course of action as it made it all the more difficult for Darren to get and keep a regular job when he left school. A friend got him his first job at his own workplace.

Over the years, because he knew what it was like to be on the outer, Darren has developed an empathy for the left-outs in life, joining groups that help people, and church activities that reach out to others. He particularly likes leading church services in aged-care facilities. His parents are immensely proud of who Darren has grown to be. Louise says that she could never have managed all those years without the loving help and support of Kevin.

Now married with a toddler of his own, Darren is the one who does both the shopping and the cooking in his household. That way he can ensure without fuss that he eats what he needs in order to be the person he is. For he knows well the old saying, 'You are what you eat.'

Misbehaving Badly

Laraine and Greg

Dr Ben Feingold was coming to town. He was a paediatrician who specialised in treating children whose behaviour was labelled 'hyperactive'. Laraine had never heard the term 'hyperactivity' but many of her friends had rung to tell her of Feingold's impending visit and that she and Greg should go along. Some had even stuffed flyers about the lecture in her letter box.

Laraine begins the story. 'We bought Feingold's book, *Why Your Child Is Hyperactive*, and read it together and discussed the possibility of going to hear him. Greg was eleven at the time. On the day of the lecture, Greg was late home from school. I was furious. "Why are you so late? Where have you been? What have you been doing?" I demanded. Greg told me that he had taken his bank book to school that day, and called in at the bank on the way home to withdraw money to pay for the lecture "because it's all my fault that we have to go," he said. How does that make a mother feel?'

*

As a baby, Greg slept peacefully all the times that a good baby would. Practically as soon as he began solid food, his behaviour changed. Laraine says, 'He's probably the only child to be suspended from kindy! A phone call came one day to pick him up early as he was disturbing the other children as they rested. By the time he was in Year 2, he was often out of control. His eyes would glaze over, he'd become agitated and aggressive.'

Later, Laraine was to learn that certain foods set off this behaviour, particularly anything with red colouring and everything that contained salicylates.

Greg's school report cards were always the same – he could do better if he tried and concentrated. But he couldn't sit still and didn't like being indoors. He drove his teachers mad for it takes just one misbehaving student to disrupt the whole class. He knew the headmaster's office well, and his cane. In those days it was often the children misbehaving badly who had to pick up the rubbish in the school yard. Laraine says that it seemed that Greg pretty well single-handedly kept the yard clean.

In the mid-70s takeaway and junk food were not as prevalent as today and Laraine mostly cooked the family food from scratch. She continues, 'One of Greg's favourite treats was hotdogs with sauce. I would give them to the children when my husband and I were going out for dinner. A double whammy of red colouring there. The object of a treat – to induce good behaviour – inevitably turned against me.'

Her philosophy of an apple a day keeping the doctor away was an ill-fated one too. The salicylates in apples were a huge problem. And until they discovered that Greg also had an allergy to wheat and milk, his favourite breakfast was Weetbix with loads of milk and sugar – fuel for a bad start to the day.

A visit to the service station could result in hyper behaviour just from inhaling the fumes while sitting in the car waiting for mum or dad to fill it up. Laraine hadn't realised that this was a meeting place for the kids after school. No wonder he was hyped up by the time he got home.

For Laraine it was an emotionally testing time. 'Many people blamed me for Greg's behaviour. On the other hand, one headmaster actually rang the doctors and told them in no uncertain terms that it was not a parenting problem. Friction was part and parcel of life. My husband found it difficult to accept that food was the cause of our son's behaviour. Friends stopped inviting us around for Greg could be very destructive. We even took him to a psychiatrist, who was of little or no help.'

For a while Ritalin was seen as a wonder drug in the treatment of hyperactivity. Laraine tells the story of advice for medication. 'Various doctors wanted to put Greg on Ritalin, but I asked what the side effects might be. As they couldn't tell me, I refused to put him on it. We have since seen kids who were on Ritalin, and they do have other problems, so I'm pleased I didn't go down that path. Another doctor wanted to put me on Valium so that I could cope! When I explained that I needed to have my full wits about me to cope with this child, I was told to come back when I was ready for help. I had previously known one of the kindy mums who was on Valium, and she was just so spaced out that it was a worry – one can be too relaxed. One morning when we were walking the kids to kindy, she, being in front of us, ever so casually said, "Mind the snake", and kept walking right past the huge snake on the path!'

*

Laraine and Greg did go to Feingold's lecture and the whole family changed their eating habits, avoiding artificial colouring, flavourings, sweeteners and salicylates.

'We began in the next school holidays when at home, making it easier to get used to new eating routines. And lo and behold for the first time Greg slept in, and then woke up without his usual fighting mood. What a relief! In the following term instead of Greg being up and annoying the family at the crack of dawn, I had to wake him up for school. And Greg was again called to the headmaster's office, but this time to be complimented on his changed behaviour.'

But constant vigilance was still needed. One day he was watering a neighbour's garden. They had an apricot tree. Greg asked before eating a couple. He quickly learnt that apricots were no good for him. He didn't sleep for two nights and returned to his horrid persona. To this day he hasn't touched another apricot, but he has overcome his problem with milk and wheat.

Laraine tells the story of a birthday party. 'For my youngest son's birthday we had a party around the backyard pool. I had ensured that all the party food was safe, but an elderly friend brought along a bag of lollies which were shared later in the afternoon. Within minutes, half the kids had become hyper, the pool had to be cleared, the party came to an early end.'

Soon after the Feingold lecture, the family moved to the United States for a stint. Here Laraine and Greg joined the Hyperactivity Society and it wasn't long before Laraine was volunteering her services for the group. On one occasion over there, Greg was peeling an orange. In so doing, skin and juice got on his hands. It was soon evident that there was something wrong with these oranges, for they had been safe food in Australia. Little did they know that at the time oranges were often sprayed with orange colouring to make them brighter, shinier and more appealing to the customer.

Back in Australia and having left school, Greg worked at a variety of jobs until he decided to study to become a chef. He married a girl who already had four children.

'The marriage didn't survive the seven-year itch,' says Laraine, 'and Greg ended up as a single parent of the two youngest kids. They knew on which side their bread was buttered – literally, as Greg was cheffing at the time. It was at this time that he realised how important it was for children to have a male mentor. And that the need is strong for male teachers. So back to more study and graduation as a primary school teacher. We went to the ceremony. We were so proud of him. Greg enjoys teaching and has a soft spot for kids who are struggling or misbehaving. After all, he has been there.'

*

Today, hyperactivity is known as ADHD (Attention Deficit Hyperactivity Disorder). Its symptoms have been well described in a couple of these stories, but today there is not so much emphasis on the Feingold eating plan. But certainly for Laraine and Greg and Louise and Darren and hundreds of other families, it changed their life.

It Never Rains but it Pours

Sheryl and Joseph and Ben

The old saying 'It never rains but it pours' seems to epitomise Sheryl and Mike's family. Plenitude is followed by extravagant plenitude.

'I used to be known as the lady with lots of kids until Joseph and Ben joined the family. Then I became known as the lady with not one but two kids with Down syndrome.'

All her life Sheryl had wanted a big family. This was also an essential prerequisite in a husband. She and Mike were happy to have as many children as God sent them. Having had three miscarriages, they now have seven, currently ranging in age from twenty-three to nine years.

'And sometimes we wonder why God hasn't sent us another baby. I really miss having a baby in the house, although I'm not sure how I would cope with yet another one,' says Sheryl, as at fifty-something she has yet to encounter the hot flushes of menopause.

When number six, Joseph, was born at home (like most of the others) the midwife kept quiet about her suspicions (she thought there might be a heart problem) but offered to accompany Sheryl and Mike a couple of days later as they took Joseph to the Women's and Children's Hospital for his paediatric check up. The midwife had planned to help Sheryl deal with whatever eventuated in the consultation but her car broke down on the way so she didn't make it. Meanwhile, Sheryl and Joseph were passed on to a different doctor, who presumed that she had been told the news that Joseph may have Down syndrome. 'It was a huge shock,' says Sheryl. 'Initially, but not for long, Joseph went from being my precious baby to being a baby with Down syndrome. Mike nearly fainted on the spot when he found out.'

One of the results of Joseph arriving a couple of weeks early was an imbalance in the air pressure of his lungs due to prematurity causing him to turn blue on exertion like sucking. Poor muscle tone caused him to have trouble breast feeding and so he failed to put on weight. On top of that he was suspected to have heart problems and even leukaemia – luckily these two suspicions were quickly eliminated. Sheryl stayed in hospital with him for a couple of days, days when the enormity of it all slowly began to sink in.

In the beginning, as Joseph didn't have a typical Down syndrome appearance, Sheryl thought that she might be able to get away with telling no one but her parents of his condition. She took him home to a family already traumatised by a car accident involving a nephew and about to celebrate her parents' golden wedding. No time for niceties of who was to be told. Joseph had to return to hospital for two and a half weeks to deal with severe jaundice and feeding problems, and to rule out liver problems and possible bone marrow problems. It took three months of expressing milk and bottle feeding before he built up enough muscle strength to breast feed properly.

Sheryl continues the story. 'When Ben came along two and a half years later, I knew as soon as I held him in my arms that he too probably had Down syndrome. For starters, he had the thick neck, short limbs and the set of his eyes that went along with the syndrome. Why? I cried, Why me? It's not fair.'

But those feelings soon went by the board as she delighted in Ben's beautiful sucking, his seeming strength and vigour and his kicking enjoyment of his first few baths. However, it soon became apparent that Ben had a congenital heart condition that needed surgery. About fifty per cent of infants with Down syndrome have a severe heart defect. Atrial-ventricular septal defects such as Ben had require open heart surgery for correction. At ten weeks old he flew for the operation with his mother at the government's expense to Melbourne, where Sheryl stayed at Ronald McDonald House for the ten days. Two and a half years later he needed a further operation to remove a flap that turbulent blood flow had caused to grow near the aortic valve.

As with all her children, Sheryl fully breast fed both Joseph and Ben for ten months before introducing solids. Sheer persistence in expressing milk for the first three months paid off, although occasionally she felt rejected by these young babies not being able to suck properly when her other five had all taken to the breast like bees to pollen-filled flowers on a sunny day.

Sheryl shares a time when it seemed like the rain was pouring. 'When Ben was born, Mike had just been made redundant, which meant that on the one hand he could stay at home and help me with the children, but on the other hand there was no income. But we knew that the Lord would provide. After three months we had used up all the redundancy payment, so Mike started his own maintenance business. Two and a half years later, a mixed blessing intervened – two elderly and dear relatives died leaving small inheritances that saw us through and enabled Mike to buy a new van for the business.'

Support for the family has been vital in helping Sheryl and Mike to cope. First and foremost, the older children in the family have embraced the two youngest sons and help in all sorts of ways. And they wouldn't have managed without the boys' grandparents, who often swapped houses for a night to give Sheryl and Mike a tiny break away together. The Down Syndrome Society of SA (DSSSA) has been vital in the lives of Sheryl and Joseph and Ben and the rest of the family. They have provided, and continue to do so, practical advice, services and resources for managing not only the two children with Down syndrome but the whole family on a whole range of issues. They also provided a forum where Sheryl could know that she would be understood as a whole gamut of feelings came and went about the joys and difficulties of raising two special-needs children.

A DSSSA grief workshop helped with bottled-up feelings that tended to blow every now and then like a pressure cooker. Foundation 21 offered funding for speech therapy after the boys started school; Disability SA had provided therapy in the early years. The Variety Club has given them larger-than-life trikes and a state-of-the-art trampoline which help the boys with mobility and balance, as well as providing much fun; and computers.

Sheryl recalls with gratitude, 'Our new church community has been supportive not only with casseroles in times of crisis but also in providing a range of further social opportunities for us as a family. One retired lady even invited the lot of us to her small unit for tea. I could talk to these people about matters of faith knowing that they would understand as they had similar beliefs. And their prayer support was invaluable too.'

Right from the beginning, Sheryl and her family encouraged Joseph and Ben to be as independent as possible. They walked at eighteen and twenty-two months respectively. Understanding and speaking language is something that has to be worked on constantly, and there have been behavioural issues, especially with Joseph. Both the boys are slow and easily distracted in their daily routines, and both, like many children, can do and say 'NO' at times.

The path through early intervention programs, playgroup and kindy to school was easier with Ben, having already walked it with Joseph. Sheryl explains, 'Every single life skill has to be deconstructed into bite-size steps to be taught to the boys – it all takes so long to achieve. Joseph is currently learning to tie his shoe laces. Have you ever wondered how many steps are involved in a seemingly simple task?'

Fiercely wanting their children to be as independent and to live lives as near to normal as possible, Sheryl and Mike campaigned their way into a mainstream primary school that was at first reluctant to accept them. Sheryl had checked out schools with special arrangements for such children and found that the cons outweighed the pros every time in comparison to a mainstream school.

Living close enough to walk all their children to primary school, the daily excursion gave everyone much needed exercise. 'Sometimes I get a sore back or elbows from towing them behind me to hurry them up so that they make it on time. Now in Years 6 and 3, the boys are slowly learning to read and understand at a very basic level, to count and compute, to fit into a group of peers both in the classroom and in the playground.'

Sheryl continues, 'Joseph and Ben each have a unique personality. They are very different, each with their own particular needs, likes and dislikes.

Joseph is very emotional and scared of heights and water, whereas Ben didn't even cry much as a baby. He just put on a distressed-looking face when hungry. Ben is kind, loving and compassionate, whereas Joseph is more pushy and demanding and more likely to use badgering tactics to get his own way. Ben is full of ideas for play while Joseph is more of a follower but then likes to take control of the game. I got out of bed one morning recently to find that Ben had made a fritz, cheese, tomato and mayonnaise sandwich for Joseph's breakfast. For the rest of the family he had cooked a concoction of coffee, cocoa, milk, chopped tomatoes and fish oil all poured over a bucket of apples. All with a very sharp knife! I reckon that their guardian angels work overtime!'

Joseph is also hyposensitive – he craves stimulation on his skin and so gets into touching trouble at school. He likes to pretend he's a dog. He sometimes growls in greeting, hides under the table or desk and occasionally licks people and things.

Sheryl finds that she is constantly tired. Being mother to just one child with Down syndrome can be a full-time job, let alone two of them. Sometimes she feels guilty that perhaps the rest of the family don't get the attention they deserve.

She makes sure that Joseph and Ben do extra-curricular activities just as their other children did. They go weekly to gymnastics and swimming, learn guitar and tap dancing. She always cooks proper meals but has learnt to live with elements of a messy house, for the energy just isn't there to keep up with the housework. She tries not to worry about the perceived judgements of other adults. The older children all have their tidying and cleaning tasks while Mike attends to the bath and bedtime routines, teaching Joseph and Ben to look after themselves in dress and hygiene, and reading bedtime stories.

Being naturally a night-time person, Sheryl finds that after tea is when she can get things done, but it's always up again at six-thirty in the morning to prepare for school. All along she has made a point of ensuring that every child had an annual birthday party with the full-themed works. Joseph had a medieval party this year with lots of relatives and friends, and he just loved it.

Sheryl tells stories of both the children running away, as often small boys do. 'At one of the older teenager's birthday party where table tennis was played in the covered driveway and the food was served inside, Ben took off in the dark through the open gate. It was several minutes before anyone noticed that he was missing. Mike organised the older children to search the neighbourhood in pairs. Ben was eventually found sitting in the middle of the road directly in front of a car with two sedate old ladies waiting for him to move out of their way.'

And 'When Ben and I were setting off at the airport for Ben's heart operation in Melbourne, we suddenly noticed that five-year-old Joseph was missing. Panic set in as it was only minutes before boarding time. We searched the departure lounge, the toilets and further afield. Eventually one of the older children found him eating a packet of chips that he had swiped and about to head out into the carpark through the front doors. Some kindly lady had stopped him from escaping further. Such was his timing that I had leave without saying goodbye.'

*

I visited Sheryl and Mike's home and found Joseph and Ben to be delightful boys who made sure I felt at ease. They finished their reading tasks on the computer, ate their dinner, gobbled up the lamingtons I'd taken, and went with Mike for their bath and bed without even a murmur. Seldom do I see such a well-oiled machine as their family functioned in their evening routine. And as I enjoyed my cuppa after tea, I reflected on what a remarkable woman Sheryl is with great inner strength that she would say is born of her faith. A faith in which Noah was definitely a role model – for he too experienced that it didn't rain but it poured. But he was kept afloat through it all. Eventually life for him settled down to a peaceful and harmonious existence too, under the protection of God's rainbow.

A Veteran Affair

Ann and John

She didn't notice it when he was first laid in her arms. It wasn't until she had rested a bit and was ready to give her son his first feed that she saw that his three middle fingers on the left hand were webbed together. 'Have they given me the right child?' she wondered. The nursing staff hadn't noticed it either. 'You'll need to take him to a paediatrician after you get home,' they said.

And then one day about a month later, when Ann had John on her knee with her hand cupped under his arm encouraging him to burp, she thought she could feel his little heart beating away nicely – on the wrong side. Another visit to the paediatrician. Sure enough, she was correct in her surmise. Later in life as he grew, she discovered that his pectoral muscle was absent on the left-hand side, a rare congenital condition known as Poland's syndrome. John was affected on the left side of his body and three bones were missing from his left hand. She wondered whether the heart had lodged itself on the protected side of his body in compensation. By now Ann was beginning to suspect that her husband's exposure to Agent Orange in the Vietnam War was being played out in her son. This abnormality has been accepted by the American government as being due to service in the Vietnam War, but only if the mother served there.

John was eighteen months when he had his first operation to correct his fingers. Skin had to be taken from his abdomen to be grafted on to the fingers. Infection set in on the abdomen site. The story was similar when they separated the other two fingers.

John grew to be a shy, reticent and unassertive child. When he was three, Ann's husband bought a business in which Ann was required to work too. John definitely did not like child care and proclaimed his distaste loudly when dropped off.

Part of John's childhood consisted of frequent and long periods in hospital with his mother when his older sister was admitted with severe asthma. Waiting in a ward with not much to do and going home in the dead of night when it was cold and wet, it was no wonder that he too caught many colds that sometimes turned into asthma attacks. Any assistance in looking after sick children was not on Ann's husband's job description as a father.

Ann continues the story. 'One day when aged about six, while waiting for me to try on some clothes at Tea Tree Plaza, John used his parka as a skipping rope. He tripped on the bulky "rope" and fell forward onto the hard wooden floor, lobbing squarely on his nose. Another trip to hospital to repair his broken nose. Sent home the next day, I noticed that during the night John woke with a spiking temperature. This time the doctor sent him to Burnside Hospital for a week of IV infusion of antibiotics as it was considerably quieter than the busy Women's and Children's Hospital.'

He had had five operations by the time he was six.

John started school at a Catholic school at Windsor Gardens. His sister started in Year 5 at the same time. Windsor Gardens was not close to home but it was necessary to move his sister from the asthma-inducing pollens of the leafy northeastern suburbs. When John reached Year 5, he found himself one of only five boys in the class; the other four had already paired off in previous years, excluding John from their games. Ann visited the school to see what could be done to improve John's position. The teacher spoke to the boys about it all; the other four boys dutifully changed their ways, and swapped partners. Still John was completely left out. So in Year 6 he transferred to another Catholic school in the region that catered for Years 6-12.

Ann says, 'It was at about this time that John became the object of his father's ire. Like many Vietnam vets, my husband was not an easy man to live with. Whatever John did was wrong, whatever John didn't do was wrong. He just couldn't win. His self-worth was battered.'

At twelve John had his appendix out, even though initially the doctors weren't too sure on which side of his body they would find it – with the heart on the wrong side, the other internal organs could have been on the wrong side too.

By Year 8 John was experiencing blinding headaches almost constantly and missed a lot of school. Then, to compound matters, sleep disturbances set in. He would sleep for up to seventeen hours at a time. On other occasions he would be awake for twenty-three hours. Who could function in a nine-to-five world with this sleeping pattern? Believing that mothers know their child best and that John's troubles were genuine, Ann took him to the doctor once again. But no one in the medical world was interested or would help because the problem was not sleep apnoea.

The next school John tried was Marden Open Access College, where he could do his lessons at home by correspondence in his waking time.

Ann explains, 'Part of the deal was compulsory attendance at a telephone conference call when necessary. This would inevitably be during John's sleeping time. It didn't work out. Eventually a doctor prescribed sleeping tablets and John went back to school, this time to Marden Senior College. After six months on this regime, which included some good work in the classroom, he would find himself falling asleep over his books. So he stopped taking the sleeping tablets and cut his classes to only those subjects that were taught in the afternoon, to accommodate his sleeping problems. We did try to address John's sleeping problems through a sleep study, which was of no help, again because he didn't have sleep apnoea.'

To escape the added pressure at home from his father's failure to understand that John had a problem – in fact, he had many problems – John left home at twenty-one to live in a rented house nearby with a couple of friends.

When John was eighteen, his father had retired and so John was able to claim an educational allowance from the Department of Veterans' Affairs. He continued his schooling until he was twenty-one but the allowance was stopped as he was only doing part-time study. He still needed to pay his share of the rent and living expenses. He was told that he had to get his sleeping problems sorted out, then he could go back to DVA-funded full-time study!

By this time, John had managed to complete a few Year 11 subjects and a few Year 12 subjects, but didn't have the magic piece of paper that would be a passport to a satisfactory job.

In the same year that her husband retired, Ann found that she had health problems of her own. She needed treatment for the non-Hodgkin's lymphoma/chronic lymphocytic leukaemia, which had finally been diagnosed in 2000, a slow-developing cancer that caused excessive tiredness but no pain.

'It was in 2005,' she continues, 'while I was undergoing yet another round of drastic treatment (haematologist's description), that my daughter, who was living and working in Canberra at the time, badly injured her knee playing soccer and had to have a knee reconstruction. Living in a third-floor flat with no lifts in the building, she needed help just to manage on a daily basis. Because of the risk of infection I wasn't able to fly interstate, so John offered to go. It was a good bonding time for brother and sister. But when he came home he found that one of his flatmates had damaged his possessions. He was devastated.'

On top of having to leave home and being cut off from his studies, John suffered so much distress that he was unable to function any more. A breakdown ensued. Ann explains, 'John became even quieter than normal, wouldn't eat, wouldn't go out, even wanted to come home again to live despite his father's continued presence there. Once more I took him to the doctor.'

Now started the rounds of being let go early in job placements that had been arranged by the employment service: sometimes because of the unsuitability of the work, sometimes because of frequent absences and sometimes because the funding ran out. Sleep problems weren't considered a condition that merited a Centrelink pension. Working for the dole was disastrous for John with such sleeping patterns.

With John's continuing woes he again visited the Veterans and Veterans' Families Counselling Service – he had previously visited them about problems with his father. This time he struck an understanding psychologist who sent him on to a psychiatrist who gave John a book in which he recognised himself and his patterns of life. It helped – John felt comfortable with this psychiatrist and has continued to consult him.

Through adversity Ann had blossomed. She began a craft group at her church to provide an excuse for women to come together to socialise. And later she started a support group for wives and partners of Vietnam vets where they could share experiences of the difficulties of living with post-traumatic stress disorder. Ann's faith and willingness to share her troubles with other women gave continued help and support to both her and the other women. And John inherited a lot of her compassion for other people.

In 2009 Ann's husband, John's father, died. To Ann's amazement, John offered to deliver the eulogy at the funeral. With his sister's help, he spoke beautifully and sensitively about how the outside world encountered his father in a whole different light than the family did at home. While the family was preparing the eulogy, each contributing their own experiences, John was strangely quiet. When pressed for the reasons, since John probably suffered the worst of them, he simply said, 'He was still my dad.'

Ann concludes by pointing out that studies of children of Vietnam veterans have shown that these children suffer from more mental health problems than the normal population. At the present time the federal government is conducting a study on the health of families of veterans of Vietnam and Timor-Leste.

The Story My Grandmother Never Told

Barbara and son*

My grandma had a baby. In fact, she had several, including one who died shortly after being born. My grandma, Barbie, never told this story. She would mention bits and pieces here and there and this is the accumulation of all these bits. I remember sitting at the table with her one day asking her how many babies she had and she told me that she had a baby that died. That's all she ever said about it to me.

My mum is the oldest of four children. She, Margie, was born when her parents, Harry and Barb, were living in Innamincka, in far north-east South Australia. Barb travelled to Adelaide to give birth, returning when the baby was about six weeks old. I'm not sure where Harry was, but being the policeman in a one-horse town probably meant he met his oldest child when she was six weeks old.

This story takes place in the 1940s, some time between 1945 when Mum was born and 1948 when my aunty was born. It was in the days of rationing and stoic stiff upper lips. One didn't share one's intimate details with anyone, not one's husband, not one's best friend and certainly not with the world on Facebook or Twitter.

Innamincka at that time was along the track to Queensland, a small, dusty, drought-ridden town with one policeman, a hospital with two nurses, a pub, a few distant landowners and some local indigenous personnel. Barb had previously been one of the nurses. After marrying Harry and being disowned from her own family (Harry was a Catholic), Barb settled into life as the policeman's wife. She tended what little garden they could raise with the bath water, milked the goats, kept a clean house and made nutritious meals for the poor

* My daughter, Nicki, Barbara's granddaughter, wrote this story. It is my mother's story.

unfortunates locked in the cells. Margie was born the obligatory nine months and one day after Harry and Barb were married. All was well. This much I know.

Here's where the speculation starts…

All was well and life continued. Barb tended the garden, milked the goats, cleaned the house and made nutritious meals for the poor unfortunates in the cells and was soon expecting her second baby. As far as we know, Barb's second pregnancy progressed as normal.

The baby came on early, forcing the decision to have the birth in Innamincka rather than travel to Adelaide. Labour, which promised to be shorter than the first, began by progressing normally. However, it soon became obvious that things were not normal. We know that the Flying Doctor was called, but due to a raging dust storm he wasn't able to land at Innamincka. The clinic sister could see that things were dire. Something was preventing the delivery of this baby. We speculate that the baby went into some kind of foetal distress and died before it was born.

Here's the horrifying part and the reason Barb never wanted to speak of this story. The baby's head had to be crushed so that it could be born. Later it was found that the baby, a boy, had hydrocephalus, which causes the baby's head to swell to an abnormal size.

Barb went on to have three more children. Each of those babies has a story too – another time perhaps. By the time my aunty was born, Harry, Barb and Margie had moved on. They lived closer to Adelaide and medical assistance.

Barb died a few years ago, taking her untold story and her grief at losing a child this way with her. The only other person who could tell this story with any accuracy would have been Aunty Rill, the nurse who had been stationed with Barb at Innamincka and Barb's best friend. She flatly refused several requests to tell Barbie's story, saying that if Barb didn't want to tell the story then it was no business of hers to tell it. A true friend to the end, which leaves us only speculation.

Sometimes these stories need to be told.

When Is a Son Not a Son?

Mary and Harold*

A genealogist sometimes unearths some anomalies in families. The family being researched today listed that the eldest of John and Mary Hall's six sons was Harold James Hall. He was born about three years before John and Mary's marriage.

Among the correspondence when Harold was wounded in World War 1 was a telegram from Mary: 'Very anxious. How progressing? Hope speedy recovery. Love Mother.' Such was his injury that he came home early from the war, and was next known to be on a farm with the rest of his family. Here he was further wounded when he was accidentally dragged along under farm machinery that was pulled by several horses.

Before this time, the genealogist had overlooked the fact that Harold was part of Mary's family, but prompted by today's generation sought to fit him in. Checking out his birth record, it was found that his father wasn't John Hall but George Mattison. The name rang a bell; sure enough, Mary Hall's father was also George Mattison. So Harold was Mary's brother, not her son at all.

So what happened to George and Rachel Mattison that their son was brought up by their daughter and adopted by her husband? Will we ever know, given that the child Harold was probably unaware of his true origins? Certainly descendants were not in the know. Rachel Mattison died when Harold was seventeen; her husband died when Harold was forty-three, so he certainly hadn't been left an orphan.

A small clue might lie in the fact that Rachel was forty-six when she had Harold, and that her next youngest had been born seven years before that. Perhaps Rachel was poorly after the birth of her ninth

* I have changed the names in this story to ensure privacy.

child? Perhaps she was ashamed of yet another child when she should have been barren by then. Perhaps Mary took pity on her mother and brought up as a son her brother who was twenty-three years younger than she. Who knows, and what does it matter anyway? It's just one of those riddles that one finds in family histories sometimes.

Old Woman Pondering

Jean and Ken*

My husband could be quite violent at times. I probably shouldn't be telling you this as he was a pillar of the community, a man of standing, a man whose job it was to help others.

It was our son Ken who copped it; he only tried the girls the once before he came to his senses about them. 'Never hit a girl' was later his advice to his grandchildren. But it seemed to be OK for him to hit a boy, especially a mischievous, full of life, curly-headed son who was always so full of adventure and fun.

The first time he really got stuck into him was when four-year-old Ken and a friend (and egger-on, I might add) made a huge mud pie in the chooks' water trough with a bag of cement and a dozen eggs. Ken's friend was spoken to severely and sent home with his tail between his legs, but Ken was locked in the woodshed for an hour 'to think it over'. Soon afterwards, Ken lit a fire in the long dry grass on the verge of the golf course over the road. The whole town had to come and help put it out. A resounding smack followed, and into the woodshed again, this time for a couple of hours.

The time that really broke me was when he got stuck into Ken with his cricket bat when he was about nine. I can't even remember what his crime was that time. Something about shooting a neighbour in the bum with his home-made bow and arrow. Whatever, it really got my husband extremely worked up. He was like that: get him in a bad mood and anything could happen. His language could be foul, enough to burn your ears off. And he really believed that corporal punishment was the only way to teach a child. Not surprising I guess, given that

---

* The basic facts of this story are true; however, fictitious names have been used. Jean has now passed on. The ponderings are probably mine.

many still gave credence to 'Spare the rod and spoil the child', and certainly his own father lived out that maxim.

But, oh the ferocity of it. He literally beat the crap out of him. Poor little bugger. It was a wonder that there were no broken bones.

And did I do anything? Not at all. I couldn't bear to even watch it, and went outside to bring in the washing but I could still hear his desperate screams.

Did I say anything? Not really. Not much more than 'That was a bit excessive, wasn't it, dear?' In those times, a woman didn't question her husband's relationship with his children or any of his actions.

Now that I have grown old and spend much time in reflecting on life and love and all those things, I realise how dreadfully wrong I was to just let it go like that. I should have stepped in and stopped him, even if meant copping a serve myself. How do you decide whose side to be on – your husband's or your son's? It seemed pretty cut and dried back then that the husband was always one's first loyalty, but now that I see how Ken still carries the emotional scars within and has never really got over it even though he's a grown man, I wonder if it shouldn't have been Ken that I protected.

I have a special spot in my heart for Ken now, and love it when on the rare occasions he calls in, for he lives as far away as possible. My husband is dead, gone to his grave without ever questioning his actions. I mean, how can you when you get dementia? Convenient, hey? But I still carry the regret, a huge and niggling lump of it sitting at the bottom of my heart...

The Boys and I

Anonymous

Watching my older son board the plane that would take him to live with his dad was heart-rending. My husband and I had separated about a year beforehand. That had been a tough year for all of us and despite my son saying to the contrary, I felt that I had somehow failed him. Another part of me recognised that he needed to experience being with his father and he had a right to do so. I had to let him go, even though deep down, I had a strong feeling he would be let down.

Our two sons took the break-up badly, with the elder, who was twelve at the time, venting his anger outwardly and often at me. The younger, eight years old, seemed to internalise his feelings so it appeared that he was coping well. Not so – later I learned that he thought that in some way he was to blame for the separation. Over time, more sad revelations were to follow.

For me, the pain of the marriage failure, watching and feeling the boys' pain, trying to be both mum and dad, moving frequently and having very little support around me, was almost too much to bear. It was like wading through mud and I felt I didn't cope; it was more like bumbling my way through each day. I made mistakes and some unwise choices. During this time, a single friend asked me, 'What are your plans for the future?' I could only reply, 'Look, mate, I'm flat out getting through each day, one at a time, let alone planning the future!' There were good times as well but I think I was too tired to enjoy them much.

The one thing I was certain of was that I loved those boys and wanted to be there for them and never give up on them. They needed at least one parent to provide stability and I knew that parent was me. I did my best but frequently felt less than adequate, and guilty for not being able to continue in the marriage and therefore placing us in this position. The responsibility I felt for this was far more than was necessary and it is only in relatively recent years that I have gotten over it.

We were forced to leave the home we dearly loved and live in rental accommodation. One thing alone would have been difficult for young boys but all things combined meant a huge adjustment for them. Their teenage years were a challenge, to say the very least, and again each of the boys had his own way of negotiating that course. Both tried living with their father at different times but those times did not work out at all well so both came back.

Neither of my sons was a criminal nor a bad person but they were angry rebellious teenagers, hell-bent, it seemed, on giving me grief. They got ten out of ten for that. One chose a certain set of scrapes, vices, mischief and so on and the other seemed to sit back and think, 'OK, my brother did this, this and this. I guess I'll try that, that and that, plus a bit more, just to make certain that dear old Mum has faced a wider range of headaches.'

To explain this fully would require something resembling a book in itself so I will just say that alcohol was a problem for one son and drugs were a problem for the other. I have no desire to dwell on these parts of their lives, nor do I wish to trivialise them. At the time they were big issues and I truly did fear for each of their lives during the peak of those complexities. The anger and resentment carried over into their adult lives and has required time, patience, communication and tears to sort through misunderstandings, misconceptions and heartache.

Many issues were dealt with as a particular situation or catalyst presented itself. However, one hurtful problem kept rearing its head and didn't get dealt with until I eventually found the courage to assert myself and bring it out into the open. I knew very well that both the boys outwardly vented their anger at me and not their father. I could understand their anger but not the way they only directed it at me.

Finally, I could take it no longer. I said, 'I'm aware that I'm not perfect. I've made mistakes and I'll accept responsibility for my part in the situation but I'll be damned if I'll keep taking it for both your father and myself.' At last I had done what should have been done quite some time before then. I believe that was beneficial and it did lighten my load.

It is easy to link certain problems to single parenting. I am thinking of the 'not feeling loved' dilemma. To my horror, I learned that both boys didn't feel loved. I felt an overwhelming sadness that I hadn't managed to convey to them how much they, indeed, were loved. I reassured them that I did love them and very much wanted them.

A while later, I was chatting with a long-time friend who had a loving husband and father of their three children. (I would add that my oldest son admired this man's fathering so much that he wished he had a dad like him.) However, my friend shared with me that recently one of her sons had said to her that he had never felt loved.

The boys and I have been over some rough tracks together but I am so glad that I stuck by them and never gave up on them. We now have healthy relationships and are friends. They sometimes share with me their disappointment in their father. This ability and willingness to share is beneficial for them.

Both the boys and I have recognised what we needed to seek help with and work on. I believe the boys have done this admirably and I also give myself some credit too. There is no value in regrets or sadness anymore. Now we can even laugh about some of the situations they got into (during the most difficult years) because it is over and in the past. The knack they both have for relating those tales makes them seem hilarious.

I am extremely proud of the people my boys have become. I love them dearly and thank them both for what they have given me.

The Birthday Party

Sandra and Stephen*

'It wasn't until his twenty-first birthday that I suspected anything,' Sandra says. 'At his party there were many openly gay couples of both sexes. Then his older sister, who was three sheets under the weather at the time, made a congratulatory speech which included a loud and raucous interrogation: "Are you gay or something?" This was the first I knew of it. It didn't bother me if he was, but it set me thinking… So I asked him next time I saw him whether he was gay. "Sort of," was the guarded and inconclusive reply. That is the one and only time the subject has ever been mentioned in my presence.'

There was nothing in Stephen's childhood and teenage years that would lead one to think that he might grow into being gay. He played sports like every other kid, but ultimately had to give most of them up because of his exercise-induced asthma. He persisted with basketball for quite some time but came to prefer the computer. He was softly spoken and reserved with adults, but talkative and very social with those of his own age. 'He was never the macho type,' says Sandra, 'but he liked the finer things in life. Ever since high school, girls have swooned about him.'

Because they lived in the country, Stephen left home at seventeen to go to uni in Adelaide. He found some accommodation through the university noticeboard and lived in a house with a group of boys, who moved on and out of Stephen's life as they graduated. Then he lived with his sister for a while.

At some time after the birthday party, for about six years, Stephen went to live with a guy who was a hairdresser. 'He was out there gay,' Sandra explains, 'with the looks and manner of what has become a stereotype. Stephen brought him home several times but the nature

* Fictitious names have been used in this story.

of their relationship was never spoken of, nor any hint given by their interactions. I never asked again, just surmised. My parents would be scandalised, but that is of their generation. The rest of our family just accept our son, brother and cousin for the nice guy that he is.'

Cool, Calm and Collected

Catherine and Matthew

The hyped-up crowd at the wrestling match booed the extraordinarily athletic masked character who could spring and somersault his way out of trouble. Meet Matthew, oldest child of Catherine.

Catherine is cool, calm and collected. Nothing seems to bother her. She has good friends she can talk to when life seems to be a bummer. She has support through her faith and her church. So she stays cool, calm and collected.

Recently a groom at his wedding was thanking his groomsmen, and said of Matthew, 'He is the most highly principled person that I know.' It seems that he stays cool, calm and collected too. Nothing much seems to ruffle him, he takes life as it comes and operates from a core ideal of not judging others.

Matthew arrived as the second grandson on his mother's side of the family. Much loved and much cherished. It wasn't long however, before he started to develop quite a severe eczema which, as it often does, was followed by asthma. There were some scary times when Catherine was racing Matthew to hospital when it seemed that he couldn't catch another breath. By the time he started kindy he was loath to leave his mother's side.

School was a breeze for both son and his mother. Matthew became very determined not to let his asthma hinder him in any way. He played football, did cross-country running and karate, never giving up when it became hard and difficult to breathe. He would just calm himself down, take a puff of his puffer and soldier on.

Herself from a family where current affairs, politics and social justice were ordinary topics of conversation, Catherine had always talked realistically to her two children about the problems associated with having a Vietnam veteran husband. Matthew took it all in his stride. Rather like Catherine's own attitude, really.

He took Art as a subject in Year 12, but left the doing and handing in of all of his assignments till the last two days before the exams. And then they were brilliant. A couple were exhibited in the Education Department gallery. Once when Catherine's beloved cat had died, Matthew presented her with a beautiful framed charcoal drawing of her pet. He went on to complete an Advanced Diploma in Visual Art, but found it difficult to find employment in the field. Catherine encouraged him into teaching, so he completed the qualifications needed to be a primary school teacher. It took a long time to attain permanent status, and Catherine remembers well years of Matt's (and her own) heartache of waiting on the day before school started hoping that there would be a phone call with a job offer.

Earlier Matt had been a lead singer for a hardcore punk band. Then he sported a mohawk, a nose ring and pierced eyebrows. Later he acquired a set of full arm tattoos. His mother nearly died when she first saw them. Now he provides the vocals for another band. The Triple J Unearthed website describes this band as having 'a never give up attitude, or simply not knowing any other way; [this band] continues to fulfil our lives with the fast hardcore punk music we need to live, breath and survive'. And yet these bands are straight edge bands, they stay clean and sober, they refrain from using alcohol, tobacco and recreational drugs – a direct reaction to the sexual revolution, hedonism and excess usually associated with punk rock and heavy metal music. Another website relates, 'These guys play blitzkrieg fast, and heavy hardcore punk rock designed to smash your ears. With insightul lyrics that cover a multitude of topics including political and other social themes.'

Encouraged by the influence of another band member, Matt became a vegetarian, and eventually a vegan. He lived at home until he was twenty-five and Catherine cooked his meals within these confines, and cooked for the rest of the family without these confines. When she started vegan cooking there was very little in the way of supermarket products to help as there is now. She herself likes meat. She says it was her insistence on him having dairy products, especially cow's milk, as a young child that probably exacerbated the eczema and asthma.

Matt has a teenage daughter from a previous relationship and is a very hands-on dad.

With a little help from mum and dad for a deposit on his first house, Matt is now living in his third property. Everything seems to be going smoothly with his new partner.

He is also into Chinese kick-boxing and wrestling. He has been wrestling for many years, and now wrestles as a masked character that the audience loves to hate and boo. Catherine, an expert with the needle, made him wondrous costumes, and with her husband, went to watch these shows and competitions, reluctantly in one sense as it is not their thing, but in another sense full of pride.

Nowadays Matt's day job is teaching Year 4 and 5. Last year he was the coordinator of student learning and guided the learning of both staff and students in improving the information communication technology (ICT) that was used in the school. His students helped him make an animated film about frogs disappearing off the face of the earth which was a finalist in a national competition, for Matt is also heavily into environmental issues. Catherine regularly teaches craft and sewing to his class. Matt has been nominated for an outstanding teacher award. One of his students goes to the wrestling matches but is not quite sure which of the masked characters is his teacher.

Catherine is very proud of her son and his cool, calm and collected path through an exciting life.

The Power of Simple Words

Anonymous

Something that I have learned over the past seven years is that words are powerful things. They have the ability to destroy, and the ability to heal. I learned this fact as my relationship with my young son went from near disastrous to one full of love and acceptance. Here is my story…

My son was planned and welcomed, and was the much anticipated first grandchild to four grandparents. My husband and I were ready for kids, having spent the first four years of our married life making the most of each other and the world.

Unfortunately (as all of us mothers now know), what we imagine pregnancy, birth and life with kids to be has no relationship to reality. In my mind, everything was going to be perfect. I was going to love pregnancy, the birth would be natural and I would adore spending time with my new child.

Pregnancy was spent in and out of hospital with unexplained bleeding, numerous drugs, two weeks confined to bed and a back that didn't know whether it should align to the right or left. Birth did not come when expected but was ten days late. In the end, my son was born by emergency Caesarian, having the cord lying across the birth canal and wrapped around his head twice and having a very big head.

The first ten days went by well as my son slept, as most young babies do. At eight weeks, things began to take a turn for the worse as we noticed that he was always hitting his head and ended up scratching himself until he bled. Visits to doctors determined that he had eczema – and thus the nightmare began…

Our son would cry virtually every minute he was awake. He would only ever sleep for forty-five minute intervals (night and day). My husband and I would take shifts through the night. The only thing that would settle him was to sit him in our arms and raise him up and down, up and down, up and down, while pacing the house. When we did put him down in his cot, we would have to sit next to him holding his arms down so that he did not scratch his head till he bled. We tried gloves and wrapping him up, but he was an escape artist. He never smiled, just gazed at us, almost accusingly. He was not easy to love.

Over the next year, regardless of how much he could understand, I told him that I wished I had never had him. The relentless routine, day and night, lack of sleep, lack of reward (oh, how I wished he was cute rather than covered in red, ugly eczema – and if he'd only smile…) made me understand how women who don't have a support network can commit the ultimate, unforgivable crime. Luckily for me, I had family and friends around me who knew to drop everything as soon as they heard the sob on the other end of the telephone.

When my son was old enough to start on solid food, the reason for his temperament and eczema became clear, as it was obvious that certain foods were highly allergenic to him. After enduring months of what must have been agony, he was finally diagnosed with numerous, severe food allergies. Once these things were removed from his diet and mine (as the allergens pass through the breast milk) things began to settle down, although I still didn't feel the close bond with him that other mothers and children seemed to have.

When he was two, our daughter arrived, and you couldn't have imagined more of a contrast. She was cute, happy, smiled all the time and was engaging and adorable. I found myself shunning my son and resenting the fact that giving time and attention to him meant that I wasn't able to be totally absorbed with my daughter.

The pattern of resentment and guilt continued for the next four years, until one day the contrast between how I treated my daughter and how I treated my son became apparent to me. It was a night that, while it was completely ordinary in most ways, will stay with me forever. I remember tucking my son into bed and giving him a hug and a kiss. I then went over to my daughter, tucked her in, gave her a hug and a kiss and told her how much I loved her. As I left the room, I turned and looked back to see my son looking at me with a look of intense longing, and at that point I realised that while I expressed my love for my daughter so openly and easily, I found it near impossible to say 'I love you' to my son.

Over the next six months I made sure that I told him that I loved him every day. At first it was difficult, not because it was a lie (because it wasn't), but because it felt unusual, but I persevered. Then eventually he started to reciprocate. At first it was notes left on my bed or under my pillow, saying simply, 'I love you, mummy'. Then gradually he started to say it.

One year on, it is the most natural thing for us to express how we feel and our relationship is stronger than ever. I love my son – I always have, but it took six years for me to discover that words were what we both needed to heal.

Christmas Story

Mary and Jesus

Every year afterwards they told my story, mothers to their children and priests to their congregations, in plays and in processions, and in all languages. And while most know the allegorical nature of my story, the way it is told makes it sound like a bed of roses, without the thorns, some fantastic pain-free episode of great joy. So let me give you an idea of what it was really like.

*

I was tired, so tired that my bones ached. Especially my backside. All that sitting on our donkey, even with blankets beneath me. And it was getting dark. We seemed to have taken so long to get here, what with having to stop every couple of hours so that I could take a wee behind a bush. Even that was fraught with embarrassment – there were so many people on the road all moving towards Bethlehem that it was difficult to find a private bush anywhere. We'd come across the hills from Nazareth, three days' journey. The donkey had been patient and consistent, but camping out in such cold weather was not much fun. If only the Roman emperor wasn't so keen to get wealthy quickly, we wouldn't have had to all go to our husband's home town to be counted, so that the emperor would know how many of us can pay extra taxes.

Joe had been pretty good. He'd walked all the way. He must have been tired too, right to his sore feet.

And now here we were in Bethlehem and already we'd been to several pubs but no one had any spare beds. And while not due for a couple of weeks, my contractions had started. I guess all that bumping around for three days unsettled the flow of things within. We needed somewhere to spend the night so that the baby wouldn't be born on the street. Even an animal shed would do.

And so it came to pass that I settled down on a bed of prickly hay that made me sneeze all the time. All night my contractions kept coming, hard and fast. It was cold and wet outside while inside cows were mooing and pigeons cooing all the time, not to mention the stink of freshly laid animal dung. It was almost more than I could bear. The publican's woman was trying hard to act as midwife, but didn't seem to know too much about the birthing process. But she brought cloths and hot water, and drinks for Joe. His concern and company were crucial for me to keep on keeping on.

I'd seen enough births to know when to push. The time came in the early morning just as a weak sun was pinking the clouds. So push I did and out came a slippery baby boy who wailed with full voice. The publican's wife gave a scream of fright and ran out of the shed, so Joe, despite being a mere male, had to do the catching, the wiping and the wrapping in swaddling cloths before I put the child on my breast. And then he had to clean up the mess.

We called him Jesus like the angel had said.

I was just beginning to get him and me settled when there was a knock on the shed door, and in walked a couple of dirty and scruffy-looking shepherd families, with a tiny lamb and a toy drum in their hands. 'We heard about your boy from the angels who were in the paddocks singing Glory to God, and we decided to come and see the dear little thing. Sorry we had to bring the sheep with us. They'll be all right outside.' So they pulled back his covers and gooed and gaaed into his face. He opened his eyes and looked at them. At least that's what they liked to think. They were on about a saviour, just like the angel was all those months ago. I'm a bit short on understanding all of that right now – at present, Jesus is just my tiny and precious newborn.

Then later in the evening along came three princely-looking gentleman in long flowing cloaks all covered in dust as though they had just made a long journey through the desert. They too tied their camels to the hitching posts outside; you could hear the camels snorting and spitting away out there. Their gifts were very mysterious: gold, frankincense and myrrh. What on earth did they mean? And what was I to do with them? 'We have seen this birth in the stars which we followed from far away places. And we have come to worship him. And to warn you that Herod wasn't too happy to hear about the birth of this little king. We would warn you to get away quickly and to flee to some place that is well out of his reach.'

So we up and left in the darkness of that night with our brand-new baby and me hardly recovered. Back on the donkey's back and off at a trot. Where was the joy in all of this?

We hadn't got an hour out of the place when we realised that in our haste we had forgotten to register our name on the census. Oh well, that's life.

www.ingramcontent.com/pod-product-compliance
Lightning Source LLC
Chambersburg PA
CBHW021838020426
42334CB00014B/686